I Laughed When I Wrote It

Wrote It

518 of My Funniest Tweets

Alan Zoldan

Zoldan, Alan
ISBN: 978-0-7443-2379-5
I Laughed When I Wrote It: *518 of My Funniest Tweets* /
Alan Zoldan – 1st ed.

SynergEbooks
948 New Hwy 7
Columbia, TN 38401
www.synergebooks.com

Printed in the USA

I LAUGHED WHEN I WROTE IT

DEDICATION

To my darling wife Elaine, whose quirky sense of
humor is, um, quirky.

ACKNOWLEDGMENTS

I want to thank my family – Elaine, my one-in-a-million and ever-supportive wife; my children and children-in-law Joey and Malini, Michael and Michal, and Melissa and Ben – it is one of the greatest honors and pleasures of my life to be your dad and watch you grow into such phenomenal people. You are all incontrovertible proof that your mom and dad did a few things really well – or just got really lucky.

Of course, there are all the "little people"– my too-cute-for-daycare grandchildren. Levi, Beth and Shimon, you don't need jokes to laugh, and your sweet laughter is sunshine to my heart; brother Merrill, also terminally afflicted with the Zoldan funny gene, sister-in-law Lisa, nephew Corey and niece Robin (who will announce this book on her vast Facebook network if I ask cousin Melissa to ask her).

Hugs and fist bumps to all my first-rate friends: Austin and Heidi, Jeff C. and Lori, Norman and Robin, Jeff H. and Laurie, Lenny and Leah, Steve, Ed, and Alan – long may we run. To paraphrase the late, great Zen Master and Hall of Fame catcher Yogi Berra, thank you for making this book necessary.

On the business end of things, many thanks to Debi Staples at SynergEbooks; Cindy Mich, my publicist; and for every funny movie, TV show, book or comedian that ever cracked me up. To paraphrase the late, great Zen Master and Hall of Fame catcher Yogi Berra, thank you for making this book possible.

TABLE OF CONTENTS

INTRODUCTION

*"They all laughed when I said I'd
become a comedian.
Well, they're not laughing now."*
– Bob Monkhouse

*"Comedians are sociologists.
We're pointing out stuff that the general public
doesn't even stop to think about,
looking at life in slow-motion and questioning
everything we see."*
– Steve Wright

If you wrote 500 and some odd jokes, would people read them and laugh? Would it even be possible to write that many quips?

In a nutshell (a walnut shell if you demand specifics), that's the premise of this book. But it didn't start out that way. As a writer with a keen and unique sense of humor, if I say so myself (and I just did), I would often have comic ideas sparked by things I read, things people said, the news, the media – pretty much anything. I didn't go looking for comedy fodder so much as comedy fodder material seemed to be looking for me.

The problem was (although some of my friends would assert that it wasn't a problem at all) I seldom wrote down any of my jokes. From time to time, I would share them with friends and family, but more often than not they simply evaporated, like steam from a wet road on a hot summer day.

And then came Twitter. Not being a social media junkie, I had no desire at all to broadcast my every waking thought (or deep dark secret) to strangers, followers, and strange followers. On the other hand, the new messaging platform did offer three excellent features that might hone my comedy writing chops:

1.   Twitter would give me an easy-to-access place to write and store my jokes. As long as I was within reach of my iPhone, I could tweet to my funny bone's content.

2.   The 140-character tweet limit (now 280 characters) was perfectly suited to my preference for writing succinctly. Like they say, brevity is the soul of wit. Actually, it was Shakespeare who said it – in *Hamlet.* Ah, the sublime joys of being an overeducated, underemployed English major!

3. Presumably, Twitter would give me the opportunity to expose my creative efforts to the world. That, I must confess, has not aligned with my reality-be-damned projections. To date, I have no fewer than of 48 beloved followers – hardly the dent I had hoped to make in the Twitterverse.

That was the game plan, and – oddly enough – I stuck to it. I did not tweet on a regular basis. Sometimes weeks went by between tweets, sometimes months. And then there were periods in which I was a comedic dervish, spinning out seven or more threads of comedy gold within days.

My point is that this was a no-pressure project for me – no deadlines and no quotas to meet. Nobody in the world – including myself – was pushing me to do this fun little side project. I started doing this in 2011, and with no real expectation that my pile of tweets would ever evolve into a book.

Seven years and 895 tweets later, I began to think that I might have enough material for a book. A joke book. *This* joke book. And indeed I did.

You might wonder why there is such a discrepancy between the above number of tweets and the 520 jokes that appear in this book. In a word: editing! I expunged all the quips that were too similar, too tasteless or offensive – although I'm sure you'll find more than a few that are. And that's okay. If I don't offend at least some of you some of the time, then I'm really not doing my job. What three people find offensive might make 33 other people guffaw.

I deleted other jokes because they now seemed less funny or more arcane than they did at the time. Other jests did not make the final cut because they did not age well. Their humor was contingent on some topical event that I could not reasonably expect the typical reader to recognize or remember. And once you have to explain a joke (all together now, class): it's no longer funny.

Finally, you might wonder how I got to be so darn hilarious – or in what cruel world do I even think I am? First of all, I'm not pretentious enough to believe that the whole world will explode with laughter at my stuff. I'd *like* to be that pretentious, but I'm not there yet. Comedy is very much in the mind of the beholder, and I have enough difficulty mapping the nooks and crannies (especially those crannies!) of my own mind to be bothered much with yours. Hell, we haven't even met!

I can tell you, however, that these tweets were funny to me (hence my self-explanatory title), and I figured that would give them a reasonably good chance of tickling your fancy. Besides, as my sainted mom always taught me, sharing is caring. And I wanted to share my very best.

I hope you find these 520 tweeted jokes – or most of them – as funny as I did – and maybe even funnier. After all, they're coming to you enhanced by the element of surprise, and you didn't have to suffer the tedium of polishing them.

Unfortunately, these are debilitating, disheartening, and disquieting times. Laughter may not be the solution, but it can be a balm, a stress-reliever, and some sunshine for your soul. As a famous person I just made up once said:

"We need more love.
We need more sex.
We need more laughter.

We need more kindness.
We need more gratitude.
We need more connection.
We need more joy.
We need more serenity.
We need more hope.
But most of all,
we need more cowbell."

Alan Zoldan
Wesley Hills, NY
February, 2018

LAUGHING @MYSELF

G.V. Tenuta

"Laugh loudly, laugh often, and most important, laugh at yourself."
~ Chelsea Handler

"Laugh at yourself first, before anyone else can."
~ Elsa Maxwell

Have you ever noticed how some of the most despotic, egotistical, and just plain nasty people in this world have an almost pathological aversion to laughing at themselves? The way I see it, you can spend a ridiculous amount of time, money and energy trying to maintain a glossy but razor-thin façade of perfection, but sooner or later you're going to join the all-too-imperfect human race. And crash landings hurt, so why not just take yourself a wee bit less seriously?

All the tweets in this chapter are about me – but they are not necessarily about the real me. Some are based on real things in my life, and some are just for laughs – so why do I say that they are about me? Because they are all, to one degree or another, *self-deprecating* – jokes that poke fun at oneself...or at least at one's persona.

Researchers in Spain recently found that laughing at yourself could be healthy, with such benefits as enhanced happiness and sociability? No joke. You can find the article at http://www.dailymail.co.uk/sciencetech/articl e-5369579/Self-deprecating-humor-good-study-finds.html.

One of the researchers, Jorge Torres Marín, explained the work: "In particular, we have observed that a greater tendency to employ self-defeating humor is indicative of high scores in psychological well-being dimensions such as happiness and, to a lesser extent, sociability."

It's been said that he person who knows how to laugh at him or herself will never cease to be amused. I couldn't agree more. After all, we are the human condition writ small, and while there is certainly much about our lives that is serious, sad, scary, inspiring, mundane, tranquil, pulse-pounding and more, there is also a component that begs to be laughed at. Our pretentions. Our embarrassments. Our faux pas. And even our pas faux.

These are serious times, but we don't have to be relentlessly grim about it. Laughing at ourselves – or me – can be a great way to deflate our egos and recalibrate our perspective. *If you can laugh at it, you can live with it.* Anyway, that's what often works for me.

(1)

Damn – my new Practice Patience app is taking FOREVER to install!

(2)

If breathing counts, then yes – I multi-task.

(3)

Last weekend, I went to the mattress. Naps. Reading. Scrabble on my iPad. It was a good weekend.

(4)

I'm sick of being a hypochondriac. Hey, wait – I'm cured!

(5)

I seldom judge people – except, of course, those people who are always saying "Don't judge me!" That's pretty much asking for it, don't you think?

(6)

I don't judge people generally. I judge them very specifically.

(7)

I like to send some of my friends get well cards and gifts even when they're well – just to mess with their lack of gratitude.

(8)

I started a nonprofit organization once – but not on purpose.

(9)

23 years in the copywriting game and I still haven't managed to use the word "quotidian" – until now.

(10)

I'm sure what you're saying is very interesting – just not to me.

(11)

It really sucks that my spirit guide from the future won't tell me any football or basketball scores.

(12)

Playing Words with Friends would be great – if I had any.

(13)

Seasoned global traveler? Not really. But I am quite well known at my local International House of Pancakes.

(14)

I could never be a rambling guy. The roaming charges alone will kill ya.

(15)

Have YOU seen my glasses? I'm running out of options here.

(16)

They made me wait one hour for my stress test yesterday. My attitude was like – didn't you guys just give me one?

(17)

Yeah, I buy books from Amazon and then return them. Am I cheap? Sleazy? Or am I just making Amazon my bitch?

(18)

My friend told me that he thought I was being unduly influenced by all the violence on movies and TV – so I shot him.

(19)

They stole my identity, but I'm so full of self-loathing that I'm paying them to keep it.

(20)

The other day I think I had a near-life experience.

(21)

I'm thinking about having my spirit animal put to sleep.

(22)

The license plate on the car in front of me said
PLSSMILE – which I sure did as I tailgated him
like white on rice for the next 13 miles.

(23)

When my GPS recalculates my route, it always
sounds passive aggressively pissed off.

(24)

I read yesterday that interrupted sleep
stemming from breathing disorders may
increase the risk for Alzheimer's. Didn't get
much sleep at all last night. Thanks, Readers'
Digest!

(25)

I used to like it when my wife acted like a baby
in bed – until the time she started wailing and
crying for about half the night.

(26)

I really tried to follow my passion, but
apparently there are laws against stalking.

(27)

I went viral last week. No joke – the flu can really kick your ass.

(28)

If I wasn't running repeatedly from my driveway to my home and back for my keys, and/or my glasses, and/or my phone, I'd be getting no exercise at all.

(29)

My son offered to take me out for Father's Day. He says lunch will be on him – kind of like when he was two.

(30)

Maybe it's just me, but why does the person in front of me with the overflowing shopping cart NEVER bag his or her groceries?

(31)

My daughter-in-law is a germaphobe. "It's nothing to sneeze at," she says.

(32)

I went viral last week. Sadly, it had nothing to do with the internet.

(33)

I have a drug test scheduled for next week. I wonder which drugs we will be testing.

(34)

If joining in with the IHOP wait staff to sing Happy Birthday to some astonished and uncomprehending 3-year-old is wrong, I don't want to be right.

(35)

I think it would be funny to die while taking a "how long will you live" quiz.

(36)

I once tried to market black onyx rings as mood rings for chronically depressed people. It didn't work – but then again, neither did the rings.

(37)

I think I'd make a good sugar daddy. I'm already diabetic.

(38)

So I read this article the other day, "50 Things You'll Regret On Your Deathbed." I thought there should be a 51st: wasting your time on that stupid article.

(39)

This year, I have decided to just give up for Lent.

(40)

43 people are following me on Twitter, and I don't even feel paranoid about it. The meds are working.

(41)

Sure I have better things to do with my time than amuse you with witty tweets. I just can't think of any at the moment.

(42)
I've learned to lower my expectations as I go
thru middle age. It's called LOSING.

(43)
My new voice mail message positions me as
the hip smart-phone-savvy dude that I am. It
says: "Please hang up and send me a text."

(44)
Doesn't take too much to ruin my day -- like
when the supermarket cashier doesn't thank
me for bagging.

(45)
My new "economy" dental plan – just chew on
of one side of my mouth.

(46)
I can accept almost anything, except people
who say, "It is what it is."

(47)
Please don't tell me to have a nice day. Most of
the time, I've made other plans.

(48)

Got back to my car 10 minutes after the meter expired and did not get a ticket. Life is really starting to work for me.

(49)

People don't talk much these days about the ultra-ambiguous ending to The Sopranos. Maybe it's time to move on.

(50)

I work well with others when they leave me the fuck alone.

(51)

Lost my mood ring last week. Can't even tell how I'm feeling anymore.

(52)

My idea of a balanced diet is eating chocolate with both hands.

(53)

Smartphones are cool and all, but I will wait in line overnight to be one of the first to own the world's first smartass phone.

(54)

Those toilet brushes you find in most bathrooms? They're way too rough, right?

(55)

You only think we need to talk. In reality, we must prolong this uncomfortable silence.

(56)

Nobody likes me, but that's probably because I'm not on Facebook.

(57)

I am the artist formerly known as Alan who???!!!

(58)

I have a pretty wild uncle, so I guess you could call me a Nephew of Anarchy.

(59)

So the lady in the bakery gave me a free apple turnover. Could this be the sign I've waited for to prove that the universe owes me a living?

(60)

I like to put one if my items on the other side of the dividing bar on the checkout line. It's my way of getting people to try new things.

(61)

It's getting to the point where five or more tweets represents a pretty productive day for me. Oh God, I need help!!!

(62)

I've been working on my road rage for some time, and now I've gotten to the point where I'm just road pissed.

(63)

So I liked all kinds of cereal when I was a kid. And then one day my mother gave me shredded wheat. And I was like: "This is a joke, right?"

(64)

I tried speed-dating on speed, and I got this weird kind of paranoia. It felt like all these women were not coming after me.

(65)

I'm sorry, but I'm just not going to reflexively apologize over every little thing anymore.

(66)

Past life regression? No thank you. My current life regression is challenging enough.

(67)

I need to get a life – or at least a new Facebook identity.

(68)

My career has been a kind of ad hoc cautionary tale.

(69)

The sign on the store asked if I needed an extra pair. I did – but they were only selling glasses.

(70)

If I knew a girl named Alice and gave her a chalice, I bet I could write a pretty cool song.

(71)

I often stand up and cheer for "home runs" that are just long fly outs. That's right – I'm a premature gesticulator.

(72)

So I bump into this person I haven't seen in 10 years, and he asks if my wife and I are still together. Gee, thanks for the vote of confidence!

(73)

I don't know exactly how or when, but I'm pretty sure that I've become a hater. It just seems to be the more sensible position.

(74)

I've been eating Value Meals for years, and my net worth is still the same.

(75)
Craigslist ad: "I want to write a book about my weight loss."
Me: I want to vomit.

(76)
My life goal was to live off the residuals from my being a child sitcom star in the eighties. And, unfortunately, I had no backup.

(77)
I no longer text, I just Ouija board – I find that I meet much more interesting entities.

(78)
My wife says we don't communicate enough, but she's wrong – I email her all the time.

An Australian newsreader once found himself interviewing the Dalai Lama, so he told him the joke about the Dalai Lama who asks the pizzeria to make him one with everything. And the Dalai Lama really, really didn't get it.

And I hear that the man is pretty woke. But it really has nothing to do with intelligence or having achieved a transcendent state. It has to do with cultural context. Either the Dalai Lama had never ordered a pizza with toppings, or perhaps he was profoundly aware that he was *already* one with everything – it's hard to say. And, in any event, it wouldn't be funny.

If I told you the funniest joke in China, you would probably not get it, even if I told you in English. That's not to say that the joke wouldn't be hilarious to millions of people – just that they would be *Chinese* people.

If the cultural context is not shared, then you probably won't get the humor. And context is a tricky thing, even for us "Amuricans." Where we grew up, where we've lived, how old we are, which aspects of pop culture are we more into (movies, sports, music, curling) our industry and occupation – they all affect cultural context.

So. if I you want to guess what Bob Dylan, the Super Bowl, corporate gobbledygook, social/political issues, The Sopranos, Breaking Bad, Jewish holidays, stupid clichés, social media madness, self-help hype, corporate language harassment, and Ted Talks have in common, the answer is – not a hell of a lot – but they all have been comedy fodder, deftly distilled into this chapter's jests.

(79)

I got my medical marijuana card last week.
And I've already forgotten where I put it.

(80)

The most use I ever got from a self-help book
was using it to balance my wobbly table.

(81)

I just read this great book on decluttering your
life, and it inspired me to throw out all my self-
help books.

(82)

I need an app that will prevent me from buying
more apps.

(83)

There's such a thin line between being an
interesting person and being a person of
interest.

(84)

As it turns out, my current lifestyle is
unsustainable.

(85)

I voted for Obama last week, and, sadly, my life remains remarkably the same. I am so over politics!

(86)

Today millions of Muslims begin their haj. I thank them for giving me one of my favorite Scrabble words.

(87)

I was around in the eighties, but I never even once Wang Chunged.

(88)

Hey, I'm as big a fan of breasts as the next guy – but pink shoes on NFL players? Come on!!!

(89)

Where can I get a list of all those companies that call me all day and say nothing whenever I pick up? I have a very special offer for them.

(90)

I believe in a woman's right to choose – except when it comes to rejecting me.

(91)

You know those restaurants that serve all their drinks in mason jars? They should all just stop.

(92)

I think America would be a less troubled country if people started using words like "moxie" and "jeepers" again.

(93)

There's nothing like entering contacts on a new cell phone to make you realize how few people in the world you feel like talking to.

(94)

Killer debate line for a candidate to use: "I am the one who knocks."

(95)

My doctors are optimistic – but I think that's mostly because they're rich.

(96)

Would I like sparkling water or tap? Keep me
dancing on the precipice of magnificent
uncertainty, why don't you?

(97)

I had a candidates' debate party once, but I
only invited top-level political analysts. I called
it a political master-debate party.

(98)

The iPhone 6 is so four years ago.

(99)

Sad but funny: someone at a Bob Dylan
concert, instead of clapping or holding up a
match, raised his cane.

(100)

Great untaken name for a band: Destiny's
Uncle.

(101)

I'm looking for a way to monetize being broke -
- but first I need to know what "monetize"
means.

(102)

I give major props to Steely Dan for not
licensing their song "Black Friday."

(103)

Idea for an inspiring Channuka tale: a down
and out junkie regains his faith when his
dwindling supply of dope magically lasts for 8
wasted nights.

(104)

Bob Dylan's next commercial song deal should
be with Trojan Condoms: "They say that every
man needs protection."

(105)

I went to a concert of a well-known Grateful
Dead cover band and they were selling drugs
in the bathroom -- Flomax mostly.

(106)

Sitcom Idea: A teen pop idol gets into one wild, wacky adventure after another. Working Title: Leave It to Bieber.

(107)

Do you think Bob Dylan has ever looked in the mirror and thought, "Once upon a time, you looked so fine?"

(108)

As Kinky Friedman once wrote, "There is a time to live and a time to die and a time to stop listening to albums by the Byrds."

(109)

"17 Caught in Search for Ariz. Deputy's Attackers," the AP reports. Which is good news – because I only shot the sheriff.

(110)

Paranoid people should all sign up for Twitter. That way their fear that they're always being followed would be more reality-based.

(111)

If Bob Dylan wants to license a few more of his songs for commercial use, I think these songs of his could be very lucrative: *The Answer is Blowin' in Febreze, Don't Think Twice, It's T. Rowe Price,* and *It's Alright Ma, I Just Need Tampax.*

(112)

A few more Dylan songs that could easily be commercialized: *Hey Mr. Allstate Man, Visions of Johansson (SodaStream Take 2),* and *Pokerman* (for online poker).

(113)

My idea for a Zen billboard: IF YOU WERE PRESENT, YOU WOULD BE HERE NOW.

(114)

I went to a concert of a well-known Grateful Dead cover band and they were selling drugs in the bathroom – Flomax mostly.

(115)

I don't see what the big problem is about tweeting while dr—

(116)
Are insomniacs more woke?

(117)
I try to keep an open mind, but too much
extraneous shit
keeps falling in.

(118)
I just tried to use one of those Forever stamps
in 2825, and there wasn't even a post office
anymore. Fake stamps!

(119)
I'm very psyched about the market potential for
my new app for losers. It's called the iCan't.

(120)
There's a candy store at my local mall named
"It's Sugar!" – probably because "It's
Obesity!" just didn't test nearly as well.

(121)
Pharmaceutical testimonial you'll never see:
"Ever since I started taking FloMax, I haven't
lost a pissing contest – not once!"

(122)

Social media?! "Antisocial Media" is more like it.

(123)

If you're an obstetrician who also happens to have an MBA, do you get to call babies "deliverables?"

(124)

I understand that there are a lot of things that offend a lot of people these days – so many, in fact, that I'm actually offended by it.

(125)

Forever 21? I think that's more of a delusion than a goal.

(126)

Did the Yankees NEED Giancarlo Stanton, or did the Yankees just WANT Giancarlo Stanton?

(127)

Was that shot over your head enough of a trigger warning for you?

(128)
You know what's even worse than your being offended by someone's insensitive or hateful comments? My being offended by *your* insensitive or hateful comments.

(129)
No wonder the barber shop at my local mall went out of business. With a name like "Sweeney Todd," how could it not?

(130)
Sure I'd be happy to provide some out-of-the-box thinking on this project. What are the guidelines?

(131)
I finally met someone named Siri, and she wouldn't answer any of my questions. Very disappointing!

(132)
Looking for Kickstarter funding to market a liquefied nutrition program to health-conscious Christians – Juice for Jesus.

(133)

"For your security, could you please tell me your birthday and zip code?" For my security, I'd rather not have a complete stranger ask me that.

(134)

Harvey Weinstein sadly disproves that old actors' cliché that there are no small parts in the movies.

(135)

Trump calling OTHER people disrespectful??? [no punchline necessary]

(136)

I think there should be a holiday to counter-balance Thanksgiving: Entitlement Day.

(137)

Netscape is showing so much standup comedy these days that it's not even funny.

(138)

In his SOTU speech, President Trump called for
the removal of federal employees who
"undermine the public trust or fail the
American people." #becarefulwhatyouwishfor

(139)

I think there should be a new title for the
current First Lady: First
Single Mom.

(140)

The whole social media landscape has become
such a cesspool of insults, bile and snark that it
should be renamed "Antisocial Media."

(141)

We are WOMYN –a consciousness raising
group for radical feminists who can't spell.

(142)

Enough with that "Dayenu" song already!

(143)

So the pope was once on the cover of Rolling Stone. Like, has he ever recorded even one song or starred in a movie?

(144)

So egreetings.com is closing its doors. Would it be cruel to send them a condolence card?

(145)

Facebook Relationship Status: well it's not like we're registered or anything.

(146)

Facebook Relationship Status: oh Facebook, you don't even have enough terabytes!

(147)

Facebook Relationship Status: it's like it never even happened.

(148)

Facebook Relationship Status: what day is it?

(149)

Facebook Relationship Status: taking some time off for me. Tick ... Tick ... Tick ... Tick ... Tick ... Oh God, it's not working!!!

(150)

Facebook Relationship Status: going downhill fas— what?? Oh nothing, honey. I was just playing Scrabble.

(151)

Facebook Relationship Status: it varies, minute to minute, because I am so delightfully mercurial – and, oh yes, a teenager.

(152)

The iPad Smart Cover only covers the front because the iPads back is, you know, just too beautiful. Oh Apple, please get over yourself!

(153)

Berkshire Bank promotes itself as America's most exciting bank. Does that mean more attempted robberies, more double-stuffed Oreos, more check designs, or what?

(154)

You can't really trust those Yelp reviews, because they're written by people exactly like us.

(155)

Is there a 12-step program for people addicted to self-help books? I'm asking for a friend.

(156)

My favorite reply in job interviews when they ask if I have any questions: Yes. I was wondering how you ever manage to sleep at night?

(157)

"Hey, I don't care where any of you came from. What I want to know is: where do you want to go?" – crowd-warming bit from The Motivational Standup Comic.

(158)

I dreamed I once gave a TED talk about how to fool large audiences with pretentious bullshit.

(159)

One of the best things about visiting Fiji is that you don't have to pay to drink the water.

(160)

Costco – because having enough toilet paper for the next five years may be as close to security as you ever get.

(161)

My friends just got divorced. They just couldn't agree on which was the key principle from "The 7 Principles of a Happy Marriage."

(162)

I'm really into collecting motivational quotes, and I have to say that it's made me very successful – at collecting motivational quotes.

(163)

Two words you will never see in the same sentence: "amazing" and "webinar."

(164)

My latest LinkedIn article – "How to Get Your Business Mobbed Up," is just not having the social media impact I was hoping for.

(165)

The National Security Agency could use a spiffy tag line, something like: "We hear you, America!"

(166)

<u>Top 10 Signs That You Are Web-Wise</u> Sign #1: You aren't suckered in by lame teaser headlines like this one.

(167)

Guns don't kill people. 3D printer jams while printing plastic guns do.

(168)

Florida billboard: your wife is hot. Better fix your air conditioner.

(169)

My daughter and I saw *12 Years a Slave* and it really moved us. We are now both 100% against slavery.

(170)

Neat PC idea for Washington Redskins – change logo to a potato.

(171)

"It's not too late to have a rewarding career." Or maybe not.

(172)

One thing never to say at a bris: "Okay, let's go. Chop, chop!"

(173)

Worst song to play at a bris: "The First Cut is the Deepest."

(174)

Siri, Siri, Siri, it's like if I'm not there you don't even exist!

(175)

Hey all you people who overuse "how's that working out for you?" How's that – aw, never mind!

(176)

Kids today – they think that money grows on online transfers from their parents' account.

(177)

I joined Walkers Anonymous recently, and it's been brutal. Turns out it's a twelve thousand step program.

(178)

I had an NDE experience recently, but the only people waiting for me at the end of that tunnel were annoying dead friends and relatives.

(179)

90,000 Chinese lost their jobs this week, but it's not so bad – kids are really good about bouncing back.

(180)
Never say anything disparaging about yoga to those yoga lovers. They just get so easily bent out of shape.

(181)
Facebook: 24/7 online confirmation that virtually everyone you know is having more fun than you are.

(182)
Super Bowl prediction: upon further review of the play and umpteen replays it will still be unclear as to whether the receiver had possession of the ball.

(183)
Super Bowl prediction: almost none of the commercials will be as hilarious as their creators envisioned.

(184)
Great name for online social network for people who prefer their relationships to be insult-driven: InYourFacebook.

(185)

Great name for social network reserved
exclusively for graffiti artists: DefaceBook.

(186)

For Mother's Day, it might be nice of you to
return any one of her last seven voicemails.

(187)

They laughed when I wrote about the health
benefits of Omega-3 fish oil – but that was 130
years ago!

(188)

Ruby Tuesday CEO to step down. Now if I
could only find a good song to lead in to the
video clip.

(189)

Google keeps showing me ads for my
presumed "spider problem" as I read Spider-
Man reviews. Advanced predictive buying
model? I think not.

(190)

Nissan charges a $350 "Disposition Fee" at the end of your lease. More like an "Imposition Fee" if you ask me.

(191)

Once and for all: YES, I DO KNOW WHAT YOU MEAN!

(192)

Pfizer has announced that they are stopping research on a new drug for Alzheimer's. They're just going to forget all about it.

(193)

Really psyched about my new Existential GPS – it can help steer you clear from that profound sense of being hopelessly adrift in the cosmic void.

(194)

What do I think is the most important trend in online marketing? Stupid Linked In discussion questions.

(195)

So there's going to be a gay pride parade in Nyack this Sunday. And I sure hope everyone comes out.

'

(196)

Sign in every Carvel ice cream store: "As our founder Tom Carvel said "Thank you. Come back soon!" I'm sure glad they captured those immortal words.

(197)

"Like Carlos Danger, we also give our members special attention." ~ New York Sports Club Ad

(198)

Whenever I pass all the old folks glued to the financial news broadcast at my gym, I always feel like shouting, "SELL!!! SELL EVERYTHING NOW!!!"

(199)

Deadhead Jewish dad about his son's bris: "What a long strange snip it's been."

(200)

Dear March of Dimes, maybe if you didn't send all those dimes to everyone, you wouldn't have to do so much fundraising.

(201)

It's generally a bad idea to date someone from your anger management class.

(202)

Having a heart attack can lead to depression – which puts you at risk for having a heart attack. You're a real downer sometimes WebMD!

(203)

There's a new self-help book by a Google trainer called *Search Inside Yourself*. Sadly, I am not making this up.

(204)

As a former jogger, I can tell you: 12-step programs just don't work.

(205)
Actual billboard in New Jersey, near the Meadowlands: We've got your nutritional supplements right here!

(206)
Best 2011 ballplayer name: Coco Crisp, of the Oakland A's.

(207)
There's this new thing, "compassionate divorce." I don't get it. That's kind of like that sixties song "Killing me Softly," isn't it?

(208)
What one paint company calls "Weekend in the Country" looks to me like the color of mud. Must have been a shitty weekend.

(209)
I just found True Love on Facebook. Also Herb Love, Nicole Love,
Desirée Love . . .

(210)
If you believe that you may be suffering from social anxiety disorder, the first step is: to grow a pair.

(211)
Call me mean, but anyone who calls me "boss" gets fired on the spot. How do you like me now, ex-employee?

(212)
I've never understood why more gay guys aren't into homeopathy.

(213)
Dr. Kevorkian is dead? Damn, it's always such a drag having to switch primary physicians!

(214)
Between "whatever" and "some such shit" there's really no limit to how inarticulate you can be these days.

(215)
More on the Egyptian uprising . . . brought to you by Viagra.

(216)
If you don't have anything nice to say, maybe it's time to start a blog.

(217)
There may not be enough tattoos in the world to cover your obsessive exhibitionism.

(218)
I predict that that the rebounding economy will make dumpster diving substantially more rewarding.

(219)
If anybody sends me any more Farmville requests, I am going to burn your crops and kill your animals.

(220)

So *Essence* magazine just hired a white fashion editor. My initial reaction: OH NO YOU DIDN'T!

(221)

A literate curse: May all your Scrabble tiles be vowels.

(222)

The only time baseball players should ever point to heaven is when they have been caught stealing.

(223)

I'm thinking about having my spirit animal put to sleep.

(224)

When you get to a million followers on Twitter, do you get to stage a coup or anything?

(225)

Whatever else you may say about me, I have never disrespected the Bing. And I'm not talking about the search engine.

(226)

I just spied a bunch of Salvation Army soldiers chowing down at McDonalds. So, THAT'S where all the money goes!

(227)

I just told Google Maps where to go – it was sooooooo cathartic!

(228)

Headline they should use to announce the demise of Twitter: The Trill is Gone!

(229)

In 2020, YouTube, Twitter, and Facebook will merge into a time-wasting mega-site known as YouTwitFace.

(230)

Sorry, but I really *don't* know the drill. Don't be so damn presumptuous.

(231)

Reality TV show idea #23: So, you think you can projectile vomit.

(232)
It's enough to make you throw up: National
Eating Disorders Awareness Week.

(233)
Ask your doctor if *anything* is right for you.

(234)
People who say "too much information" often
suffer from too little capacity.

(235)
Last week, I picked up some "gently used"
confetti from the Yankees parade to give to a
friend. Ah, the life of a downtrodden Mets fan.

(236)
Map Quest really needs to start their directions
on #5. I'm pretty sure I know how to get out of
my neighborhood.

(237)
People who party like it's 1999 are so passé.

(238)

New social networking site for lawyers:
Casebook.

(239)

I'm working on a semi-autobiographical script
about conjoined twins. Or as *Variety* would put
it: I'm attached to the project.

(240)

We don't have slavery anymore in the U.S. We
have interns.

(241)

Financial experts say that gold loves bad news.
Okay, gold, here goes: lately, I've been seeing
platinum on the side.

(242)

Between Twitter, Facebook, and my blog, I'm
having a lot of trouble keeping up with myself.

RANDOM OBSERVATIONS

G.V. Tenuta

In Chapter 2, I wrote about how important cultural context is to finding something funny. And that's true – but it isn't essential. The jokes in this section are – in my opinion – somewhat less dependent on cultural or topical references. They may be absurd philosophical musings, ridiculous observations, and general tomfoolery (a word I vowed to use at least once in this book).

Full disclosure: many jokes in this chapter *do* rely on some cultural reference, or at least some knowledge of contemporary American life. How many? Honestly, I don't know. As Ralph Waldo Emerson famously wrote, "Consistency is the hobgoblin of little minds." And I'm battling enough demons as it is, so I certainly want no truck with hobgoblins.

As an editor, I'm a pretty good writer, and I can tell you this: unless you're a talented illustrator like Gary Tenuta, it's pretty hard to know where to draw the line. So, you can call my joke categorizing ability inconsistent or capricious – or even flat-out random (just like I did, in the title). I'm not going to be offended because . . . well, because you're right. I originally tweeted these jokes in completely random order. And then, as editors are so damn wont to do, I was asked to organize my material into chapters – in the interest of making it more reader-friendly.

So I did. Did I do a decent job? I think so. Did I do an amazing job? Hardly. Let's just say that I'm not losing any sleep over it. Nor should you.

(243)

One sign you're in a toxic relationship: those empty little bottles of poison you find scattered around your house.

(244)

For those of you who maintain that you can't have it all, I direct your attention to: The Everything Bagel.

(245)

This is not a retweet but an original tweet that I sent back one minute into the past.

(246)

I have gone from road rage to road miffed. Today, it's just about gently honking the shit out of one slow-ass driver at a time.

(247)

HAIL SATIN!! Misspelling or bold fashion prediction? You be the judge.

(248)

HAIL STATIN! Misspelling or grateful person with high blood pressure? You be the judge.

(249)

Just wrote the best tweet ever, but it was 157 characters – and hell no, you don't edit brilliance!

(250)

My new Existential GPS is awesome. It's the only one on the market that answers the question "Why am I?"

(251)

If you illegally download an illegal copy of something, shouldn't that be offsetting penalties.

(252)

I just retweeted a text that I emailed to myself last week – and nobody cared.

(253)

Once you get beyond your pretensions, you may be running a little too far ahead of yourself.

(254)

Are you awesome or self-absorbed? Careful – most people get this one wrong.

(255)

I just don't get ambulatory surgery. Call me old school, but I think patients should be still and unconscious.

(256)

If we all knew what went into McDonald's special sauce, the world would be a less magical place.

(257)

The one line all Marvel Comics villains have in common: "Your insolence shall avail you naught!"

(258)

That parking lot they paved over Paradise in the old Joni Mitchell song? I think it badly needs to be repaved.

(259)

The best way to double your money: fold it over and put it in your pocket.

(260)

FYI: having all your ducks in a row makes you a much easier target.

(261)

There is such a thin line between aggressive marketing -- and stalking.

(262)

Dear "Hip" Marketers, please don't call your customer base a community." It sounds nice, but you're really not fooling anybody.

(263)

If you own a pair of $1200 gloves, are you any less likely to lose them?

(264)

Why is it that many waiters will ask you four or five times during your meal if everything is OK -- and yet are nowhere to be found when you want your check?

(265)

It's been a darker world since the SkyMall catalog folded.

(266)

Just saw the word "awesomest" on a store sign -- because, apparently, the word "awesome" is no longer awesome enough.

(267)

Everything happens for a reason. And that reason may be just to annoy you.

(268)

It's a sad day when you realize that YOU have become that annoying old driver crawling like a snail in front of you.

(269)

People can't drive you crazy if you don't give them the key. I feel bad for all the leftover Christmas stamps that are used in January, February and March.

(270)

I saw a license plate on a Maine truck that said "Semi Permanent." How is that even possible?

(271)

In my chronic war against the pesky squirrels who feast from my garbage cans, I am pretty sure I'm losing. They just seem to want it more.

(272)

Is it possible to binge watch without feeling a sense that you probably could be doing something better with your life?

(273)

My friend said she could never accept robots replacing people. I told her that, for me, it would depend very much on which people.

(274)

If you're an obstetrician who also has an MBA,
do you get to call babies "deliverables?"

(275)

Federal agents marching into the White House
– now that would be a grand parade!

(276)

Sauna sign: PROLONGED PRESENCE IN SAUNA
COULD LEAD TO OVERHEATING." Well, *duh.*

(277)

So if the temperature shoots up 70 degrees
after plummeting 80 degrees, would that be a
bipolar vortex?

(288)

I don't think there's a better book to keep in
your car than Jon Kabat-Zinn's "Wherever You
Go, There You Are."

(289)
Sign for a mini-storage company: Because your personality should be the only reason nobody visits your apartment.

(290)
People who say "scen-ar-io" instead of "scen-air-io" sound a lot more like they know what they're talking about.

(291)
So they rejected my tagline for the psychiatric hospital: "It's an insanely great place to be."

(292)
Car dealer's ad says "We'll treat you like family" – like this is supposed to be a good thing??

(293)
Coolest title ever for a pro bowler's auto-biography: "That's How I Roll."

(294)
Sure you can ask me a question. In fact, you just did.

(295)
People who insist on using weird spellings and pronunciations of their names need to wake up and smell the KaFee.

(296)
Ironically, most people misuse the word ironically.

(297)
Sadly, Dipping Dots has not changed the world as much as I thought it would.

(298)
Yes, we know all about your mother issues, but guess what? You weren't exactly all rainbows and chocolate sprinkles either.

(299)
Your phone messages are about 67% less amusing than you think.

(300)

Shouldn't there be some kind of cardio benefit just for wearing a training bra?

(301)

The first scratch on a new car -- how quickly life returns to normal!

(302)

Sign at my local garage says "repairs while you wait" – what other
option is there?

(303)

People who say AY-SAP instead of A-S-A-P aren't nearly as hip as
they think.

(304)

You don't know me Amazon. You just know what I'm probably going to buy next.

(305)

You know you're a real baseball fan when you see a butterfly fluttering by and your first thought is: knuckleball.

(306)
You know you're old when your daughter talks about "back in the day" referring to the early nineties – and she's right.

(307)
What do we want? Mindfulness! When do we want it? Now!

(308)
How can a man max out his cell phone data plan every month yet acquire so little wisdom?

(309)
People paid Trump University big money & got screwed. So doesn't that make it pretty much the same as any other school?

(310)
So the NY Times finally printed the F-word. It's about fucking time.

(311)
People who meditate a lot are full of sit.

(312)
The keys to a good relationship are communi-
cation and not keeping score. That said, you
should never communicate that you're keeping
score.

(313)
If I wasn't always reading quotes about
mindfulness, maybe I'd be more present.

(314)
The only people who can use the word
derivative in a non-snooty way are calculus
teachers.

(315)
It's just a guess, but I think people who say "I
hear you" are probably a lot more likely to
take a bribe.

(316)
A man in China jumped to his death after his
wife insisted on shoe shopping for five hours.
The *NY Post* called it *shoe-icide*.

(317)

I've never understood why those kids who are helped by the Make-a-Wish Foundation never wish to get cured.

(318)

If you're keeping score in a relationship, you probably have already lost.

(319)

I don't see anything wrong with people with a narcissistic personality disorder that a good long look at themselves wouldn't fix.

(320)

I have a new exercise program for depressed people. It's called going through the motions.

(321)

Does anyone know where I can get *The Complete Idiot's Guide to The Complete Idiot's Guides?*

(322)

If the answer is STILL blowin' in the wind, wouldn't it be pretty darn weather-beaten by now?

(323)

No, we're not on the same page. I don't even think you know what book I'm reading.

(324)

I wouldn't say we're in a passive aggressive relationship -- but I wouldn't say we're not.

(325)

I get enough exercise just pushing my luck.

(326)

I'd be happy to provide some out-of-the-box thinking on this project. What are the parameters?

(327)

When one door closes, it may be time to look for the nearest window.

(328)

One of the hardest things in life: getting rid of a broken recycling bin.

(329)

Great name for a takeout noodles joint: Pasta la Vista.

(330)

If not now, then soon. And if not soon, then we never eat at this restaurant again.

(331)

Say little, but move your hands a lot.

(332)

Never hold a grudge against others – unless, of course, you don't like them

(333)

What if my true purpose in life is to serve as a tragic example to others? God believes in atheists – it's the agnostics He's unsure about.

(334)

How do I handle change? I usually put it in a small box on my dresser.

(335)

If you're lactose-intolerant, does that make you a milkist?

(336)

When my daughter was 10, she already knew that there was only one thing boys really wanted: PlayStations.

(337)

They told me to get help. I am now holding help hostage.

ONE LINERS

G.V.TENUTA

I hate Russian dolls, they're so full of themselves.

If at first you don't succeed, skydiving is not for you!

My wife and I often laugh about how competitive we are.
But I laugh more.

Do you smoke after sex?
I don't know. I never looked.

I think of one-liners as the molecules of comedy – a very succinct joke or witticism, usually no longer than a line or two. It may be the shortest line from a comedian's mouth to a chuckle or an amused smile.

Most of the jokes in this book would qualify as one-liners, so, you might wonder, what's so special about the one-liners in this chapter? I'd love
to give you a wise or at least a wiseass answer, but instead I can only feebly but honestly confess: I don't know.

I just thought that "One-Liners" was a cooler title than "Miscellaneous" or "All The Stuff That Didn't Fit Elsewhere." Don't you? Anyway, I'd much rather write jokes than [SAT word alert:] turgid over-analytical explanations. **You know what's not funny?" Chris Rock once asked.**

"Thinking about it."

(338)

One thing your rabbi will never tell you: I'll see you . . . In hell!

(339)

One thing your surgeon will never tell you: you're dead.

(340)

Sure I'd take a bullet for you -- over to forensics!

(341)

I found this humerus. C'mon, throw me a bone!

(342)

I woke up this morning, and I'd already written the first line to my next blues song.

(343)

Does your iPad screen have that "not so fresh" look?

(344)
"OHHHHHH!" "OOOOOO!" "UHHHH!" –
agonized withdrawal cries of a kid who's been
hooked on phonics.

(345)
Best answer to "May I ask you a stupid
question?": You've never needed my
permission before.

(346)
Please listen carefully as my meds have been
recently changed.

(347)
Talking to your imaginary friends does not
count as networking.

(348)
I'm trying to get my cool idea for a watch
designed – but who has the time?

(349)

That "RECALCULATING" on my GPS is always so passive-aggressive – because YOUR WAY obviously didn't work, did it??!!

(350)

Do British GPS's have American accents?

(351)

Sure I'll love you unconditionally – when you deserve it!

(352)

Just answered a computer question for my daughter. Who's her tech daddy?!

(353)

Just once, I'd like to tell my GPS where to go.

(354)

My wife and I have nothing to say to each other – but we don't talk about it.

(355)

I ordered some Zen bumper stickers, but they wouldn't attach.

(356)

A flasher was arrested at our local museum, but he got off. It turns out that he just wanted to expose himself to fine art.

(357)

I got arrested just for having a copper can, copper sulfate, and a zinc rod. The charge: attempted battery.

(358)

Is it just me or – oh shit, it IS just me!

(359)

Do biscotti ever get stale?

(360)

My wife and I have nothing to say to each other – but we don't talk about it.

(361)

Great tag line for a towing business: Still hooking after all these years.

(362)

Yoga and me – it's a stretch.

(363)

Package copy for "Mini Bonsai Kits:" Magnifying Glass Included.

(364)

My friend is too old school for emojis. He's so unemojinal.

(365)

I'm developing an app that will have Siri and Alexa get into a catfight.

(366)

I'm not hurting anybody . . . I mean, anymore. [from *Fargo*]

(367)

I never could stay with someone with abandonment issues.

(368)

I tried to donate hope to a local children's hospital, but there was nothing left in that emotional account, so my check bounced.

(369)

For a taste of eternity, try eating a few Forever stamps.

(370)

Burning Man? More like Sunburned Man! Am I right?

(371)

She was engaged to a guy with a wooden leg, but she broke it off.

(372)

If you think there's good in everybody, you're just not getting out enough.

(373)

How is it that fat chance and slim chance mean exactly the same thing?

(374)

New study says that depression can increase your risk of heart failure by 40% – making depression even more depressing.

(375)

Do you look fat in that dress? Of course not! Do I look stupid in this shirt?

(376)

Screw "closure." I'm done with closure.

(377)

Like Lily Tomlin once said, I always wanted to be somebody, but I guess I should have been more specific.

(388)

So I flunked out of my comedy class. Don't laugh.

(389)

I'm going to open up a temporary tattoo parlor,
but only for a month.

(390)

Does anyone know how much it costs to bronze
a trophy wife?

(391)

Just burned 2,000 calories. That's the last time I
leave brownies in the oven while I nap.
@YIKAKAPP

(392)

Don't judge you?? It's a little too late for that,
don't you think?

(393)

You know how some people just love using
using French words and phrases to appear
more sophisticated? Très pretentious.

(394)

I thought fantasy football was just a gathering
for hardcore foot fetishists.

(395)

Please listen carefully, as the menu has been changed and pressing "O" will not help you reach an operator until we say it will.

(396)

It was the bottom of the Ninth at the Beethoven concert.

(397)

If I ever climbed Mt. Everest, "Ain't No Mountain High Enough" would definitely be on my playlist.

(398)

I'm circulating a petition to have all WRONG WAY signs changed to DON'T GO THERE!

(399)

There are too many personal trainers and not nearly enough personality trainers.

(400)

Why do I have a thing for sadists? Beats me.

(401)
Stealing laundry detergent: the ultimate white collar crime.

(402)
I make it a rule to never eat fish in France. It's *poisson*.

(403)
I'm on a 30-day diet. So far I've lost 12 days.

(404)
Can't remember why I took that memory course.

(405)
The future for antidepressants looks bleak, market analysts said today.

(406)
My friend Bob told me he's been feeling chipper lately -- but I'm not sure if he's talking about his friend or his mood.

(407)
If I were a cop, I would always try to arrest mimes, just so I could tell them that they have the right to remain silent.

(408)
The closest I'll ever get to the 1% is buying their kind of milk.

(409)
I have a friend who is just ridiculously particular about garnishes. He's such a pesto.

(410)
Burkas should be unconstitutional in America – because everyone has the right to bear arms.

(411)
It's so easy to needle acupuncturists.

(412)
Codependency is always having to say you're sorry.

(413)

I had to let go of an old friend the other day. Sadly, we were mountain climbing at the time.

(414)

I interviewed the circumcision advocate, but he was a bit snippy.

(415)

Who is the soggy schmuck who said, "Let a smile be your umbrella?"

(416)

I'm at my dentist and I think if these walls could talk, they'd probably say "AARRRGGHhH!!!!"

(417)

I killed a deer today, and I did it the way a real man should -- with my car.

(418)

Did you hear about the psychopathic comedian who killed at the comedy club?

(419)

So I tried speed-dating, but the meth made my mouth too dry.

(420)

It's gotten to the point where I just let Amazon order all my stuff for me.

(421)

Someone mugged me the other day with a framed canvas. It was my first art attack.

(422)

I need an interpersonal GPS, to tell me when I've gone too far.

(423)

I asked the waiter to wrap up my wrap, and he said, "We already did."

(424)

I am the one who spoils.

(425)

I told my wife that she was becoming very pretentious, and she said, "Who, moi?"

(426)

I don't drink any more -- but I don't drink any less.

(427)

I told my psychiatrist that I was invisible. He said he couldn't see me.

(428)

My hard-drinking friend can't go to AA meetings because everyone knows he drinks -- so it's already too late for him to be anonymous.

(429)

So I robbed a bank this morning and made off with a pretty sweet haul – nearly two dozen chocolate chip cookies!

(430)

"We don't serve faster-than-light neutrinos here," said the bartender. A neutrino walks into a bar.

(431)

I used to have a borderline personality, but it got better after I moved away from El Paso.

(432)

I really need to learn how to grill better. It's just one mis-steak after another.

(433)

Just sent a tweet while on a birdwatching walk. It just doesn't get any better than that.

.

(434)

My friend suffers from depression, but he's a real animal lover. So I bought him a bipolar bear.

(435)

There is now a specialty beer in my area called "Sweet Baby Jesus!" That is either perversely blasphemous or one kick-ass beer.

(436)

I was jaywalking when it hit me.

(437)
After all is said and done, there is usually much more said than done.

(438)
I should be at home . . . which is the name of a bar I discovered next
to the train station.

(439)
The results of my friend's IQ test were negative.

(440)
My bank teller offered me a new credit card the other day, but I told him that she had been pre-declined.

(441)
An SEO copywriter walks into a bar, grill, pub, public house, Irish, bartender, drinks, beer, wine, liquor...

(442)
My wife keeps complaining I never listen to her...or something like that.

(443)
Shortest Jewish Joke Ever: Two Jewish women were sitting quietly next to each other minding their own business.

(444)
If I agreed with you, we'd both be wrong.

(445)
Change is inevitable – except from a vending machine.

(446)
The last thing I want to do is hurt you. But it's still on my list.

(447)
I think someone stopped the payment on my reality check.

(448)
Is there another word for synonym?

(449)
I got fired for being a mattress tester because I wasn't very laid back.

(450)
In the news: World's Shortest Man Dies at Age 21. His life was just too damn short.

(451)
I live with a hypochondriac – and it's enough to make you sick.

(452)
After Monday and Tuesday, even the calendar says W T F.

(453)
Once, just for a second, I thought I saw a subliminal advertising executive.

(454)

I believe in making sacrifices, but only if I'm very low on the list.

(455)

"When you change your mind, I'll let you know," the psychic told me.

(456)

Book Idea: *The Complete Idiot's Guide to Being a Complete Idiot.*

(457)

I love cooking with wine. Sometimes I even add it to the food.

(458)

If at first you don't succeed – so much for skydiving.

(459)

Schizophrenic Taxi Driver: am I talking to you?

(460)
How many nihilists does it take to change a light bulb? Who cares?

(461)
How many women does it take to change a light bulb? Ten – one to do it, and nine friends to discuss it with.

(462)
How many co-dependents does it take to change a lightbulb? None – if the lightbulb really loved me, it would change itself.

(463)
Bumper Sticker for meta-mad slackers: [INSERT CLEVER SLOGAN HERE]

(464)
Bumper Sticker: I'd rather be tailgating you.

(465)
Bumper Sticker: My other car was repossessed.

(466)

The problem with going to my "happy space"
is that it never gets any cell phone reception.

(467)

The other day my wife said she wanted to see
rockets and stars in the bedroom – so I rented
Apollo13.

(468)

There is a woman in England with two vaginas,
two uteruses and, apparently, two periods.
Shouldn't that be called a colon?

(469)

I did pretty good in my Introduction to
Symbolism class. I got an @.

RATED "R"
(FOR RAUNCHY)

G.V.Tenuta

"If you don't laugh while you're having sex at least once, then you're with the wrong person."
~ yourtango.com

"Don't knock masturbation. It's sex with someone you love."
~ Woody Allen

Congratulations – you've made it to the back of the book! Kind of reminds me of the back of video stores back in the day, where they kept the "adult" videos. With the advent of the Internet and its galaxy of free porn 24/7, you can kiss those halcyon days goodbye.

Or maybe that was just me. At any rate, let me throw some cold water on your "sexpectations." There is really nothing especially salacious or vulgar about these jokes. They simply have to do with sex. And sex, as comedy fodder, is positively oozing with potential. It's a bubbling cauldron of fantasy, anxiety, vulnerability, ecstasy, shame, bliss, excitement, desire, sensuality, and insecurity . . . or maybe that's just me.

And even if you're 100% comfortable with your sexuality (go ahead and lie to yourself, I won't judge), there's still a bit of a thrill about poking fun at such a private and primal human activity. Kind of a collective "Wink. Wink. Look at how delightfully naughty we are!"

Look, I'm in no position to pontificate on today's turbulent and oft times bewildering sexual landscape. Positions are not my forte – I can barely do a Downward Dog. And, as an older, cisgender white privileged guy who came of age in the 1970's, I'll be the first to admit: I AM SO DAMN CONFUSED!

But not so confused that I've lost my sense of humor. That remains as turgid and twisted as ever . . . something we can all be thankful for.

In the movie *Closer*, a raw, riveting, and sexually explicit movie that one viewer called *"Carnal Knowledge* for the new millennium," Natalie Portman's character famously says, "Lying is the most fun a girl can have without taking her clothes off." I'm too much of a Natalie fan to beg to differ (that, and I'm not much of an expert on what would top most girls' fun lists), but I'd venture to say that enjoying a good joke or a comical situation definitely belongs in the top five.

(470)

Have you ever had sex in an elevator? I think that would be wrong on so many levels.

(471)

I asked my doctor if I was healthy enough for sex. He said i was certainly sick enough for it.

(472)

My wife and I were happy for 22 years – and then we met.

(473)

I really don't believe in meaningless sex. I mean, at the very least, it means that you've had sex.

(474)

Just once I'd like to relapse at a Sex Addicts Anonymous meeting.

(475)

If a politician talks about reaching out to his community it's no big deal, but when a sex offender says it, it's like a threat or something.

(476)

Protected sex is way too expensive. Not everyone can afford a bodyguard you know.

(477)

Midnight in Paris? Hasn't that girl made enough sex tapes?

(478)

Sad but true: my wife, apparently, will not be sexting me any time soon.

(479)

Remember when the only people who got to see a politician's penis was
a hooker or an intern?

(480)

I'm in a "same sex" marriage – and I'm heterosexual.

(481)

I never got into Twitter for the fame, money, or sex – which, as things are turning out, is just as well.

(482)

Impotence – nature's way of saying no hard feelings.

(483)

My friend just texted: what are you doing tonight? OMG – my first sext!

(484)

I asked my doctor if I was healthy enough for sex.
He said, "It depends."
"It depends on what?" I asked.
"No," he replied. "It depends on whom."

(485)

If you text only to members of your gender, does that make you a homotextual?

(486)

As a registered sex offender, I hate to be the one to tell you, but it's the unregistered offenders you really have to watch out for.

(487)

The Talmud tells the story of a student who hid under his teacher's marital bed to learn about sex. Thus did *Rabbis Without Borders* begin.

(488)

Tie-dyed T-shirt for sale at Joe's Crab Shack says "Peace, love, and crabs." That last one was the deal breaker.

(489)

Hey you physicists hunting for so-called Dark Matter – I don't think there's any room in science for such racism!

(490)

Like Mitt Romney, I also have a "binder full of women." But I think that one's preferred method for organizing one's pornography collection should be a private matter.

(491)

Sign on the local massage parlor takes truth in advertising to a whole new level. It reads: Thank You for Coming.

(492)

The sign on the store asked if I needed an extra pair. I did – but they were only selling glasses.

(493)

Is it okay to grope yourself? I'm so confused.

(494)

"Masturbation Symposium" – let's get to the topic at hand.

(495)

Half of adult Americans have used a vibrator. My guess is that would be the women.

(496)

I think the best security system for a bra factory would be a few carefully placed booby traps.

(497)

Foreplay is a little over-rated, I think – but *fiveplay* . . .

(498)

So my uncle was arrested for procuring a certain kind of Chinese bear for perverted purposes. That's right – another charge of panda-ring.

(499)

Talk to my doctor if I experience erections lasting four hours or more?? Yeah, like I'm gonna waste that on a doctor's visit.

(500)

It would be cool if there were a Jamaican proctologist named Pokemon.

(501)

Dear Penthouse, I never thought it could happen to me – and I was right.

(502)

They say that the key to a happy marriage is for the wife to be like a whore in bed, but I disagree. Her rates are also very important.

(503)

I'll admit it. I was kind of disappointed to learn that Groupon wasn't some kind of online swingers club.

(504)

The Kiss Cam at CitiField is no longer doing it for me. I think I'm ready for the Foreplay Cam.

(505)

Something about tribadism just rubs me the wrong way.

(506)

I don't know what you call it if you mix Viagra with scotch, but I bet that's one stiff drink.

(507)

Dear Followers, please stop sending me all those nude pix. I'm not that kind of tweeter. And seriously, your lighting sucks.

(508)

I offered to send close-ups of my male organ to random women. Thanks to all who replied that a 7X zoom might not be enough enlargement.

(509)

You don't have to be a porno actor to get a little behind in your work.

(510)

I really don't know why they call it a happy ending. I always found it more bittersweet.

(511)

Need to discreetly pleasure yourself? There's a sound setting for that.

(512)

Slogan for the Colonic Lovers of America: We're less full of shit!

(513)

If it weren't for the economy, I wouldn't be getting fucked at all.

(514)

Great promotion idea for the producers of
Circumcise This: 10% off gets you 10% off!

(515)

Working at home, I always look forward to my
solo holiday party, where I often wind up in a
dark corner taking advantage of myself.

(516)

My doctor told me that I had to stop mastur-
bating. "Why?" I asked. "Well, for one thing,
I'm trying to examine you."

(517)

They found him in his bedroom, stiff as a board
– another tragic Viagra overdose.

(518)

I kid you not – there's a specialty beer on the
market now called "Sweet Baby Jesus!" Hey,
I'm Jewish and even I was offended.

ABOUT THE AUTHOR

Alan Zoldan is a work-at-home freelance copywriter who lives in Wesley Hills, NY, with his wife and several of his descendants. He credits his mom, growing up in the Bronx in the sixties, his Jewish heritage, and heavy exposure to TV and movie comedies, iconic stand-up comedians, SNL, *MAD* magazine, Robert Crumb, HBO and Netflix comedy specials, YouTube, funny books and all his wiseass friends for developing his comedy flair. And he also *blames* them for the very same thing. Alan deeply believes that this is the book America needs at this time.